Author: Warwick McFadyen
Title: 21 + 4
      – Poems

©2023 Warwick McFadyen

ISBN: 978-0-9944362-9-0

The moral rights of the author have been asserted.
Photographs ©2023 Warwick McFadyen

Published by PB Publishing
PO Box 19
Gisborne Victoria 3437
www.pbpublishing.com.au

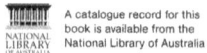
A catalogue record for this book is available from the National Library of Australia

Cover picture: Detail of a beach where the author and his family spent many enjoyable holidays.

To Pip and Grace
and
without him, and within us,
Hamish

Contents

Life in a Word • 1

Deeper • 2

Compass • 3

Sleep/Awake • 5

On Seeing • 6

Two Zeroes • 7

If, 2023 • 9

Map • 11

The Ledge/The Swimmer • 14

River/To The Ocean • 16

The Light That Travels • 18

Autumn Twilight (For Peter) • 20

Artificial Intelligence/It Could Be Anyone • 22

Glint • 23

A Graveyard on Anzac Day • 25

Airs and Grace • 28

The Harvest • 30

Easter Sunday • 31

All These Things • 32

Threads of Light • 33

The Weight • 34

Flow • 35

The Wake • 37

Listen • 38

21 + 4

Poems

Warwick McFadyen

Life in a Word

Each word to you
is a breath
I give in return,
as thanks, as prayer,
as the hand
outstretched to bring
silence close.

For time takes in
and takes out
the air that fills
the cupped voice.
And language born
of the wind
must follow its
rise and fall.

I give in return
each word to you.
And as I breathe
slant of light
and shadow
define the words
I give
in return
for you.

Deeper

How to mine the deeper meaning
I asked a magpie on the wing.
It trilled an answer air on air
that in its notes I could not sing.

How to mine the deeper meaning
I asked the lapping of the wave.
It rose and broke upon the shore,
the ebb and flow was all it gave.

How to mine the deeper meaning
I asked the weathered rustling leaf.
It bowed and bent with sighing breeze,
Time is a thief, time is a thief.

How to mine the deeper meaning
I asked the stars overhead.
They said when our light touches you
know in the parting are the dead.

How to mine the deeper meaning
I asked the rain and earth and stream.
They replied, in the life of one
dwells another. Love is the seam.

Compass

To hold a compass in my palm
and watch the needle stay true
while winds sing a ragged psalm
O, wanderer, we thought you knew

Even to eyes cast northward bound
even to the southern bands
the lines of sight stay not ground
like time-weathered marks on your hands.

The direction to a life borne
is cloaked in shadow and light
the heartbeat of the hours drawn
into the wash of your life's flight.

But the compass, I tell the wind,
lives within and shapes the road.
It is the sky and soul twinned.
It is the seed, the harvest sowed.

From earth risen a rustling laughs:
the magnetic lines of their
own are not your guiding paths
but streams of us that course through air.

And still then the compass is held
for bones are not skeletal
when breath is life, and the weld
of heart and mind defines the call:

The eye of the needle is me
From north, south, east and the west
It is the sky, it is the sea,
the stillpoint to the wind's tempest.

Sleep/Awake

When lids draw shut and eyes
in their flickering fall
into night's embrace
then we float at mercy
of currents turning
comets to water
turning water to canvas
of sky and horizon.

And awakening in this dream
life, sunlit and moon caressed,
time worn from first cry,
we are its pupils,
the painter and painted.
Each breath a brushstroke
of time, flaring and fading.
Eyes open, eyes shut.

On Seeing

For a few minutes
I stare at the points
of light, flaring
and blurring
into the blackness.
For a few minutes
I reach out and
run my fingers
over their life
and death.

For a few seconds
I allow myself
a smile to infinity,
drink the last dregs
of my coffee
And go out
into the day,
knowing those
13 billion years
will always be there.

Two Zeroes

From zero to zero
we span a little thread
vibrate to the sigh
and shout,
the wail and whisper,
kiss and caress.
We are the tremor
in the air that in the
moving is moved.

How can the sum
of it be zero
isn't the question.

The shadow
of our sway
will in time
seep into the
waiting sky,
become the fabric
we once looked
into, and
we
will
be
gone.

How can the sum
of it be zero
isn't the question.

Between two zeroes
was the touch
of the hand
against the clouds,
the trace of a name
in the echo of a
chain of voices,
in the space
between two zeroes.

If, 2023

I pushed apart
the i and f,
though they be close,
and stretched out the space
like this

i   f

I pressed my hand in to the
gap and held it there to feel
the caress of possibilities
that
        float
                within
but the letters slid back
with nary a shrug nor sigh;
though we be small,
they seemed to say,
the paths you see
the doors ajar
the rivers rushing
to the sea
the if I do, if I did
if I had done
are the constellations
shimmering in our eyes,
our can is major
and can is minor.

In the shape
of their shadow
cast, in the flicker
of their light,
in the form
is the meaning,
in the word
is the world;
opening
and
closing.

Map

The world was on the wall
of the classroom.
Mercator was its name.
The earth pinned flat —
oval frames of creation
reference points —
was the span
of my child arms.

Meridians travelled
over bodies of
land and water
wrapping the globe,
like a gift,
in the certainties
of a mapmaker's
measurements.

I placed my fingers
On the places
Where one day I said
I would go.

One day,

One day.
The lines were
a projection.

And then I was
in the world.
Each route I took,
each path I trod,
each breath,
was a mark on a map.
Straight lines
and circles
settled under the skin.

There the past resided,
going about its business.
Rising now
and again
to say you wouldn't be here
if you hadn't been there.
One day.
One day.
The lines were a projection

Of destination and departure,
an atlas of distance
the traveller takes
and does not;

of lands unexplored,
voices unheard,
whispers unmet,
touch unexplored,
eyes unopened.

On the Imago Mundi,
birds end not their flight,
the light is brighter
than sunrise and sunset;
darkness enfolds,
beasts roam
and dawn comes.
The lines were a projection.

This then is the map
within and
without you.
The lines on your face
and hands,
the words that rise
from valleys,
that skirt the sky
from mountains.

The Ledge/The Swimmer

I watch the surfers
take off
over the ledge
fall into the wave
breaking
over their shoulder.
I can see
the line of ocean
drawing itself
to the waiting shore,
the symmetry of sky
merging into
the aqua music,
the glissando
of swell
become surf
then surfer.

In that moment
my eyes fill
with the light
that turns
on the tide.

A surfer takes off
over the ledge,
for joy
for dear life.

In early light I stroke
the surface of the
sea-gathered pool,
each ripple I send
to the waiting rim
falls back on itself
and cannot ascend
over and beyond
the path I swim.

But here I know
in the water calm
and in the tow
of my path, in
the glide of my arm,
in my drawing of breath
love is both ebb and flow
of ocean and pool;
in its currents there, I go.

River

I am walking on the river bed
for the river no longer flows.
Now it feels the wind and sun
And falling moonlight's glow.

Now under the dry surface it holds
onto the thing it once had been;
the rhythms, pools and stillness,
all to the world unseen.

This is the land of droughts and flooding
rains. This is the landscape passing
within, of ripple and swirl
fading, then vanishing.

Each life is a river.

To the Ocean

In the shallows of the shoreline,
I bend to the water and gather the sea.
It slips through my hands from its time
of leaving. I cannot hold it close to me.

On the worn path in the forest,
I walk with the sun and gather the light.
It brushes my skin, and then falls
away. I cannot keep it within my sight.

And yet these moments are landscape;
my horizons, atlas of flickering line.
On sand, still wet, I write a life
in one letter, hold it forever with mine.

This is reflex of emotion.
This is the tide running.
This is the ocean.

The Light That Travels

It was bin night — yellow and green
I placed them on the kerb
and, walking back to the house,
I looked up into the night sky
and tried to read the stars
left to right and back again;
a stream of centuries' light
had travelled to me in the blackness,
in the ordinary rituals. On bin night.

Thank you, I said, as quiet as star dust.
I knew my words could not rise
to the stars. They fell fading to earth
Or were borne away on a swirl of air.
They stayed with me; a pulse,
an echo in the heart's chamber.
The stars that night were not mine,
though I held their distance close;
Scientists may give them names,

While we see what we dream
them to be.

On bin night — yellow and green
I looked up into the night sky
And knew that even as one star dies,
its light still travels through
the emptiness and nestles
in hollowed out bone
behind eyes that once looked up.

Autumn Twilight
(For Peter)

The day was folding into night
as I walked the streets of my town.
The sky fading from blue to black
was slipping on quietude's gown.

Not a sound, but the call of birds
creased the air. I could not sing
their lullabies, for I knew
their melodies they did not bring

to me. The lights of homes began
to shine in the passing windows
as in the gathering dark
more stars would come into show.

For now, a crescent moon seemed
to hang by an invisible thread
alone but for one star near — not
to guide but to the heavens to wed

the light that is carried to us
with the light in our eyes -
that in this inhalation of day's
waning, we breathe a sky's

stillpoints of wonders
and become alchemists
of beauty, blessed to have
been both star and moon kissed.

Artificial Intelligence/It Could Be Anyone

The five had given up the ghost.
Not for want of trying, they cried
but the house now was not a host
how could they stay if it had died?

Though a frame still stood to the sky
its skeleton was not a soul
while it stood upright to the eye
in the bones a ghost whistle told

of whirl of words that rose and fell
in the rotation of the day
that carried once what hearts could tell
of life and not be cast away.

Now walls bare and windows clear
marked where the senses of the realm
had been, shadow lines, broken sphere
rhythm of the saints overwhelmed.

Now the earth was flat, its orbit
in the silence of gathered gloam
beyond return, senses split
from what held them together: home.

Glint

The wash of the moon
dream-limned
from a million eyes
streamed in
and brushed
against my face.

Awakened, I asked,
What is it that
you came to visit?
The moon replied,
This is not a love song.
I've brought you this:

It's the dust
God shook off
his great coat
after he had stopped
arguing with
his younger self.

It's the particles
of worlds
that vanished

before time
had a face
recognisable.

It's the numbers
of the universe
broken up
by the tremor
of a bird's
beating wing.

It's the grain
that floats
among the stars
come to rest
as the glint and grit
in your eyes.

These things
are the fading
and the thrum,
the shadow
and the light of life.
Listen, see, speak.

A Graveyard on Anzac Day

In Gisborne graveyard
the leaves are falling,
from acorn to oak,
the seasons are calling
to each of us, a leaf
in the breeze,
a whisper in time,
a tear to the seas.

In Gisborne graveyard
the soldier stands head
bowed, his body cast
forever to mark the dead.
On this Anzac Day, he is
among headstone and grave
a sentinel among the quiet
multitudes of the same dark wave.

In Gisborne graveyard
Two women kneel to place
flowers by a plaque; they
embrace, lean in face to face.
One waters the roots
for a longer life, they must,
one supposes, while the other
brushes away the dust.

Airs and grace

I walk the airs
of early morning.
The song of magpie,
caw of crow
and cockatoo,
the burble of the creek
in its rushing
between the deeper
scouring when the current
slows and sound
bides its time,
these are the rhythms
playing on the sky,
a notation on the wind.
Into this a stillness
falls onto my skin.
I can feel its rub
as it seeps into
the bloodstream,
is carried into
the chambers
of the heart.

This is nature's valve
where silence and voice
become the pulse
of memory, and are
released into the day.
This is the soul's air
and grace.

The Harvest

It's the season of growing
and the paddocks are brown.

The colour of faith is undimmed,
yet the paddocks are brown.

It's the time of renewal
and the dams are all dry.

The call to trust is unshaken,
yet the dams are all dry.

It's the season of unfolding
and the earth it is cracked.

The heart is still full,
yet the earth it is cracked.

Easter Sunday

The bones of Christ were long gone
to dust, the ripples of the waves
said to me as I walked the shore.
And as I walked, my footprints
dissolved back into the sand,
just like time's work on the bones,
the waves whispered, the moon
and the tides could not be denied.
The sun was on the horizon,
just rising, carrying its distance
in the heartbeat of the day.
On this day death became a question
where was thy sting when ascension
transformed the white of the waves
to hands raised to the waiting sky?
But the bones of Christ were long gone,
returned to carbon, became the matter
of stars that shone into infinity.
And so I walked the shore, and felt the sun
on my skin, warming me, going deep,
deep into the wash of my bloodstream.

All These Things

The wind wild and ragged,
the sky a splintered flag.
A voice that remains
in a pool of light
The stars each a shard,
the earth underfoot.
A voice that remains
in a pool of light
The river, raft of time,
each grain of sand a beach.
A voice that remains
in a pool of light.
The mist nestling soft,
the slumbering day.
A voice that remains
in a pool of light.
The whisper of a cloud,
the heartbeat travelling.
A voice that remains
in a pool of light.

Threads of Light

At the rising of the sun while
the morning still is sleeping
and the air carries the colours
of the day in its keeping

I stand at the water's edge and
let the tide softly sing me
its moon rhythm, ripple within,
hear the murmur of the sea

like a thread in the undertow
whispering against the night:
the grace notes of life are the stars,
forming into threads of light.

The Weight

Who knew that ashes would weigh the same
in your arms as when you held him as a baby.

You hold them close to your chest,
your heart breaking, this is not something

you were expecting, to be sent back 20 years
to the cradling of love, small soft body
against yours now an emptiness of sky
heavy on your breast.

Each breath is a word, spoken or unsaid,
but what can you say as you place him
in a snug shovel-dug hole in the earth
but keep warm, my beautiful boy.

We brush the plaque now sitting over him
with our fingers - a kiss goodbye of love.
We take a small jar of him home with us.
We have his smile, we say in tear-mist breath.

That night a light rain falls and I think of him
alone in the damp earth. You are not alone I say.
You are not alone.

Flow

Empty this into my heart –
The sky, the infinite surface,
Let me feel when I look within
That I am looking out as well.

Empty this into my heart –
The wash and whorl of the sea
Let me feel the tide's pull and push
To moon light and shadow.

Empty this into my heart —
The light of distant stars
That I might hold close the wisp
Of time that I can say is only mine.

Empty this into my heart —
The whisper of wind on worn stone
That I can listen, and return it in a voice
Fulfilled, never emptying.

The Wake

The surface breaks and in the parting
lines of ripples slip away.
They crest then fade into the fold
that swirls and sleeps under the spray.

This is the lapping of each moment
from rock of cradle to silent grave,
this is the voice that no longer travels
but for what it left and what it gave.

This is the widening wake, carrying
the echo and call of a life now past
to my shore-bound days. The water
runs through my hands. I hold it fast.

Listen

Imagine the voices of the world
Now silenced rising
From the earth,
like early morning mist,
wisps of calls, looking
for echoes before
burning off in the sun
and fading out.

Imagine the voice of one
falling, as if no longer
a feather on the wind,
but into the darkness
enfolding
that is the cradle
of stone and soil
and silence.

These passing notes,
this staff of souls, this ascending
and descending,
this lightness,
this weight
of being human.
Listen.

21 + 4

About the author

Warwick McFadyen is an award-winning writer and editor based in Melbourne, Australia.

His previous volume titled The Ocean, a meditation on grief in prose and poetry, received emotional tributes on publication in 2022.

www.ingramcontent.com/pod-product-compliance
Lightning Source LLC
Chambersburg PA
CBHW051554010526
44118CB00022B/2703